TO:

FROM:

THE STRANGEST SECRET

HOW TO LIVE THE LIFE YOU DESIRE

Based on the Motivational Speech Heard by Millions

EARL NIGHTINGALE

Sourcebooks, the colophon, and Simple Truths are registered trademarks of Sourcebooks.

Photo Credits
Internal images © end sheets, non-exclusive/Getty Images; page xxiv, Westend61/Getty Images; page 4, Ryoji Iwata/EyeEm/Getty Images; page 8, Martin Barraud/Getty Images; page 24, Stewart Cohen/Getty Images; page 28, JAG IMAGES/Getty Images; page 30, Ratstuben/Getty Images; page 36, Hero Images/Getty Images; page 38, Thomas Barwick/Getty Images; page 46, Adam Taylor/Getty Images; page 60, Carina König/EyeEm/Getty Images.
Internal images on pages xx, 10, 14, 18, 20, 50, 52, and 62 have been provided by Unsplash; these images are licensed under CC0 Creative Commons and have been released by the author for use.

Published by Simple Truths, an imprint of Sourcebooks
P.O. Box 4410, Naperville, Illinois 60567-4410
(630) 961-3900
sourcebooks.com

Printed and bound in Singapore.
OGP 10 9 8 7 6 5 4 3 2 1

Table of
CONTENTS

FOREWORD
by Dave Ramsey

v

PROLOGUE
by Diana Nightingale

xiii

INTRODUCTION
by Crysten Cornish of Nightingale Legacy

xxi

CHAPTER 1:
What Is Success?

1

CHAPTER 2:

The Secret Is...   11

CHAPTER 3:

Believe and Succeed   21

CHAPTER 4:

You're in the Driver's Seat   31

CHAPTER 5:

The Price of Success   39

CHAPTER 6:

Start Today   53

TAKE THE 30-DAY CHALLENGE   63
RECOMMENDED READING   67
ABOUT THE AUTHOR   69

FOREWORD
by Dave Ramsey

Earl Nightingale was a national treasure, plain and simple.

Before there was Dave Ramsey or Tony Robbins, there was Zig Ziglar. And before there was Zig Ziglar, there was Earl Nightingale. His influence as the grandfather of motivational speaking has had a powerful impact on everyone in the personal development space, and his words and teachings have touched more lives directly and indirectly than can be counted.

I'm grateful to be listed in that number.

My parents first introduced me to Earl's message in the 1970s. They were in the real estate business when I was a kid, and they would take me to motivational seminars. I would also listen to cassette recordings of incredible speakers like Earl. So I had already been exposed to *The Strangest Secret* by the time I was twelve years old.

Interestingly, that was also about the same time that I started my very first business, mowing lawns around my neighborhood. I don't know if Earl inspired my first taste of entrepreneurship as much as my dad's insistence that I start earning my own money, but I wouldn't be surprised if his words had at least some impact.

As I grew, so did my appreciation for Earl. I remember getting the chance to hear him speak in that wonderful baritone voice at the Municipal Auditorium in Nashville, Tennessee. That day, he shared the stage with some real legends: Paul Harvey, Zig and Judge Ziglar, Cavett Robert, and Charlie "Tremendous" Jones.

What an incredible lineup!

That day reinforced so much of what I had already learned from Earl, the kind of stuff you'll learn from this book. As you read Earl's words, you're going to discover what the strangest secret in life is all about. More important, you'll realize why this has become the bestselling personal development talk in history.

And here's a spoiler alert: the strangest secret is "you become what you think about."

Now, if you're reading this book, I'm pretty sure I didn't spoil anything. You already knew that. But it's important to remember exactly what Earl was teaching through this talk. In almost every generation, so many men and women just drift through life with no real purpose. And when that happens, the power of intentionality—really paying attention to what fills our minds—can feel like a superpower.

Of course, people have tried to discredit Earl's words by misusing them. Obviously, no one's going to become eight feet tall just because they wish it were true. And, unfortunately, I can't grow more hair on my bald head by thinking about it hard enough. But when it comes to being intentional about behavior, we absolutely become what we think about.

Here's an example I like to use: If you're married, you thought about courting and dating someone. In fact, you probably put a lot of energy into planning for it. You were intentional about working that plan, and it eventually paid off! Like any success, your marriage was the result of several intentional acts that consumed your very being for a period of time.

What you thought about became reality because you were *intentional*!

Henry Ford once said, "If you think you can or think you can't, you're right." I love that quote. I believe that you can overcome adversity, temporary failure, enemies, and almost anything else if you're intentional about setting goals and willing to take the necessary steps to achieve them. But the decision to believe it's possible is always up to you.

The classic story of Roger Banister is a great example of that.

By the 1940s, the world record for the fastest mile was set at 4:01. And that's pretty much where most people thought it would stay. In fact, one medical expert even said that if someone ran a mile in less than four minutes, his muscles would collapse, his heart would explode, and he would drop dead at the end of the race. Conventional wisdom said that humans had reached their physical limit.

And, since no one believed it could be done, no one did it—until May 6, 1954. That was the day British runner Roger Banister ran a mile in 3:57, breaking the record that had stood as a barrier for nine years. He didn't explode. He didn't fall over. He didn't die at the finish line.

He also didn't hold the record very long. Another runner broke it forty-six days later!

You see, once people realized that the four-minute mile could be broken, they went about the business of breaking it—a lot. From 1954 through 1960, the record for the mile fell twenty-two times. Today, even high schoolers at local track meets can run a four-minute mile.

Like so many situations in life, the problem wasn't in the runners' legs: it was between their ears. They had to believe their goals were possible and act on that belief. As Earl said, the power of intentionality made all the difference.

When I was first starting out, I waited for someone to "discover" me. I was convinced that an appearance on a national television show or even the nightly news would create my breakthrough moment. Now, after working more than thirty years to become an overnight success, I realize that what Earl said so many times is absolutely true: *success is the progressive realization of a worthy ideal.* The incremental, intentional steps we take create the thought patterns and momentum that push us forward in life.

That's because we live in a sowing and reaping world. What you plant in your life is going to grow.

Farmers don't plant corn and then stand back in shock when corn comes up! They understand cause and effect. They aren't looking for soybeans because they know that whatever goes into the soil is what's coming out.

They also don't control the sun or the rain, but they do control the work they put in. Likewise, you can't control how God chooses to bless something, but you can control your effort and how you use what you've been given. Like I said, intentionality is important.

Earl liked to say that our minds and our lives are incredibly fertile. Unfortunately, we probably use less than 20 percent of our intellectual and emotional capacities—and too often the part we do use is focused in the wrong direction. We get all twisted up and distracted because we're human. Earl always encouraged folks to be incredibly intentional so they could be incredibly effective.

The older I get, the more I realize the untapped potential of our minds. I remember hearing Earl talk about that on those cassette tapes when I was a teen. Now, four decades removed from those recordings, I'm still learning how profound our potential is—and how it takes intentionality to create a maximum impact.

One sure sign of greatness is a lasting legacy. And Earl Nightingale's message has certainly stood the test of time. This book reflects the story of an iconic man doing an iconic talk. And the truths you'll find here are as relevant today as when Earl first put them on a flimsy, temporary acetate record for his sales team years ago.

So, read the book. Learn the power of *The Strangest Secret*. And for goodness sake, do what Earl would tell you to do: implement it! Put these principles into practice every single day.

And one more thing…take the time to listen to an audio of Earl's original recording. I promise that you won't be disappointed.

There's just something special about hearing that *iconic* voice delivering this *timeless message*.

PROLOGUE
by Diana Nightingale

In order to tell a story effectively, one must begin at the beginning and set the scene with the time, place, and circumstances. So in order to fully appreciate the impact on the countless lives—and perhaps on the very reshaping of society as we know it today—that the writing and recording of *The Strangest Secret* had in 1956, we must revisit the time and circumstances during which it was written and recorded.

Following the end of World War II, men returned

home to find jobs, and women left the factories where they had gone to work to support the war effort and returned home to assume their duties as wives, mothers, and homemakers. For all intents and purposes, life in America had settled back in to the peaceful routine that had been established by generations gone by. Each person knew the role they were expected to play in the family and in society—a role that they had been trained for from the time they were little children. Once children were big enough to pull their weight in the family, they followed in the footsteps of their mothers and fathers, learning their skills so that when they grew up, they could marry, have children, and assume their rightful roles as the scripted characters in the drama of life as it had been written long before.

While many may have been uncomfortable or unhappy with the roles they were expected to play, they continued on, living unhappy, unfulfilled lives. To do otherwise would have labeled them as a "misfit" or a "rebel," and they would have been ostracized as having something "wrong with them," so people continued to play roles for which they believed they were not suited, living lives of unhappiness, loneliness, and insecurities, dreaming dreams and having visions of living lives differently from those around them but believing that where they were was where they were supposed to be.

Stories written about those who set off in new directions to explore the world or to dabble in experimentation, like Thomas Edison, Magellan, and other legends, may have further sparked the desire for a life lived differently, but books about these men, philosophy, poetry, science, and adventure were for the most part considered nothing more than a mental escape from the "real world" and did not serve as courage to risk or break the mold to live a chosen life.

Then, in 1956, along came a man who had lived in poverty as a child and had seen war up close and personal. His name was Earl Nightingale, and he not only had visions of how life could be lived in a way that differed from the multitude, but was actually living the life that he had imagined. He was suggesting that each of us has the power, the gift, and the ability to live our lives as we imagine them to be and then went on to reveal this "secret" as to how those ideas, dreams, and visions may be accomplished by us all!

Probably one of the most impactful statements Earl made in his message was that "the trouble with most men is that they simply do not think!" This was then and is even now troubling to most. After all, men and women have been "following the followers" since the beginning of time, and this man with this recording was suggesting that it was not only okay but that we owed it to ourselves and our families, as well as to building a better society, to think about what we would like to pursue in order to become our best selves. He was not only giving us permission but was telling us that we have and have always had the power to direct the courses of our lives.

This whole premise was so bizarre that each time

the record was played, it sparked a response so great that each person wanted to have a record of their own and couldn't wait to play it for others, who, in turn, wanted a copy of their own to share!

And so it was that this simple message that was written and recorded to be played for two weeks to just a handful of salesmen sparked a new idea that soon spread like wildfire, not only across the United States but, in time, around the world, selling millions upon millions of copies and igniting a new spirit—one of entrepreneurial genius—inspiring people to think in new directions. Suddenly, a new industry called personal development was born, inspiring and inviting people to become all they wished to become simply by changing the way they thought about themselves and about life. People began changing, and so did our world.

In 1960, recognizing the growing need for this kind of information, Earl cofounded a company that would become the world's leader in personal development/success-driven audio programs, introducing such

INTRODUCTION
by Crysten Cornish of Nightingale Legacy

In 1956, the landscape of career and personal opportunity seemed as gray as the colorless shows on TV. The trajectory of life was always the same: grow up, get married; if you're a man, go to work in your father's industry, and if you're a woman, take care of the home and the children. To follow any other path would have been not only unheard of, but frowned upon.

When Earl unveiled *The Strangest Secret* to the world, it was met with mixed emotions: a melting pot of fearful negativity and hopeful inspiration. To some, the notion that a person should fearlessly pursue their

1

WHAT IS SUCCESS?

Some years ago, the late Nobel Prize–winner Dr. Albert Schweitzer was being interviewed in London, and a reporter asked him, "Doctor, what's wrong with men today?" The great doctor was silent a moment, and then he said, "Men simply don't think!"

It's about **this** that I want to talk with you.

We live today in a golden age. This is an era that humanity has looked forward to, dreamed of, and worked toward for thousands of years, but since it's here, we pretty well take it for granted. We in America are particularly fortunate to live in the richest land that ever existed on the face of the earth…a land of abundant opportunity for everyone.

However, if you take one hundred individuals who start even at the age of twenty-five, do you have any idea what will happen to those men and women by the time they're sixty-five? These one hundred people who all start even at the age of twenty-five believe they're going to be successful. If you asked any one of these people if they wanted to be a success, they would tell you they did…and you'd notice that they were eager toward life, that there was a certain sparkle in their eye, an erectness to their carriage, and life seemed like a pretty interesting adventure to them.

But by the time they're sixty-five, one will be rich, four will be financially independent, five will still be working, and fifty-four will be broke.

So of one hundred, only five make the grade! Why do so many fail? What has happened to the sparkle that was there when they were twenty-five? What has become of the dreams, the hopes, the plans…and why is there such a large disparity between what these people intended to do and what they actually accomplished?

When we say about five percent achieve success, we have to define success. Here is the best definition I've ever been able to find:

SUCCESS is the progressive realization of a **WORTHY IDEAL**.

If someone is working toward a predetermined goal and knows where he or she is going, that person is a success. If they are not doing that, they are failures. *Success is the progressive realization of a worthy ideal.*

Rollo May, the distinguished psychiatrist, wrote a wonderful book called *Man's Search for Himself*, and in this book, he says, "The opposite of courage in our society is not cowardice…it is conformity."

And there you have the trouble today: **conformity— people acting like everyone else...without knowing why or where they are going.**

In America right now, there are over forty-nine million people sixty-five years of age and older...and most of them are broke; they're dependent on someone else for life's necessities.

We learn to read by the time we're seven. We learn to make a living by the time we're twenty-five. Usually by that time, we're not only making a living, we're supporting a family. And yet by the time we're sixty-five, we haven't learned how to become financially independent in the richest land that has ever been known. Why? We conform!

The trouble is that we're acting like the wrong percentage group—the ninety-five who don't succeed.

Why do these people conform? Well, they really don't know. These people believe that their lives are shaped by circumstances...by things that happen to them...by exterior forces. They're outer-directed people.

A survey was made of working people, and they were asked, "Why do you work? Why do you get up in the morning?" Nineteen out of twenty had no idea. If you ask them, they would say, "Well, everybody goes to work in the morning." And that's the reason they do it—because everyone else is doing it.

Now, let's get back to our definition of success. Who succeeds?

The only person who succeeds is the person who is progressively realizing a worthy ideal. He's the person who says "I'm going to become this" and then begins to work toward that goal.

A success is:

▸ *The schoolteacher who is teaching school because that's what he or she wants to do.*

▸ *The woman who is a wife and mother because she wanted to become a wife and mother and is doing a good job of it.*

▸ *The entrepreneur who starts his own company*

because that was his dream—that's what he wanted to do.

▸ *The salesperson who wants to become a topnotch salesperson and grow and build with his or her organization.*

A success is anyone who is doing deliberately a pre-determined job, because that's what he or she decided to do...deliberately. But only one out of twenty does that!

That's why today there isn't really any competition unless we make it for ourselves. **Instead of competing, all we have to do is create!**

For twenty years, I looked for the key that would determine what would happen to a human being. Was there a key, I wanted to know, that would make the future a promise that we could foretell to a larger extent? Was there a key that would guarantee a person's becoming successful if he or she only knew about it and knew how to use it?

Well, there is such a key, and I've found it.

REFLECTION QUESTIONS

Ask Yourself...

1. In what ways have you been or are you currently conforming to society's expectations?

2. How has the pressure to conform to another's definition of success prevented you from chasing your own dreams?

3. What is your personal definition of success?

If the average person realized the power he wields over his life and destiny, he would live in a perpetual state of wonder and thanksgiving.

—EARL NIGHTINGALE

THE SECRET IS...

Have you ever wondered why so many people work so hard and honestly without ever achieving anything in particular, and others don't seem to work hard yet seem to get everything? They seem to have the magic touch. You've heard people say, "Everything he touches turns to gold." And have you ever noticed that a person who becomes successful tends to continue to become more successful—and, on the other hand, have you noticed how someone who's a failure tends to continue to fail?

Well, it's because of goals. **People with goals**

succeed because they know where they're going. It's that simple.

Think of a ship leaving a harbor. And think of it with the complete voyage mapped out and planned. The captain and crew know exactly where the ship is going and how long it will take—it has a definite goal. And 9,999 times out of 10,000, it will get there.

Now let's take another ship—just like the first—only let's not put a crew on it or a captain at the helm. Let's give it no aiming point, no goal, and no destination. We just start the engines and let it go. I think you'll agree that if it gets out of the harbor at all, it will either sink or wind up on some deserted beach—a derelict. It can't go anyplace, because it has no destination and no guidance.

It's the same with a human being.

Take the salesperson, for example. There is no other person in the world today with the future of a good salesperson. Selling is the world's highest-paid profession—if we're good at it and if we know where we're going. Every company needs top-notch salespeople, and they reward those people. The sky is the limit for them. But how many can you find?

Someone once said that the human race is fixed, not to prevent the strong from winning but to prevent the weak from losing.

The American economy today can be likened to a convoy in time of war. The entire economy is slowed down to protect its weakest link, just as the convoy has to go at the speed that will permit its slowest vessel to remain in formation.

That's why it's so easy to make a living today. It takes no particular brains or talent to make a living and support a family. So we have a plateau of so-called security, if that's what a person is looking for. **We have to decide how high above this plateau we want to aim.**

Now let's get back to the strangest secret, the story that I wanted to tell you today. And I'd like to begin by asking you an extremely important question:

Why do people with goals succeed in life and people without them fail?

Well, let me tell you something that, if you really understand it, will alter your life immediately. If you understand completely what I'm going to tell you, from this moment on, your life will never be the same again. You'll suddenly find that good luck just seems to be attracted to you. The things you want just seem to fall in line. And from now on, you won't have the problems, the worries, the gnawing lump of anxiety that perhaps you've experienced before. Doubt...fear...well, they'll be things of the past.

We become what we think about.

Here's the key to success and the key to failure: we become what we think about. Now, let me repeat that. *We become what we think about.*

Throughout all history, the great wise men and teachers, philosophers, and prophets have disagreed with one another on many different things. It is only on this one point that they are in complete and unanimous agreement.

Consider what Marcus Aurelius, the great Roman

emperor, said, "A man's life is what his thoughts make of it."

Benjamin Disraeli said this: "Everything comes if a man will only wait. I have brought myself by long meditation to the conviction that a human being with a settled purpose must accomplish it, and that nothing can resist a will that will stake even existence for its fulfillment."

Ralph Waldo Emerson said this: "A man is what he thinks about all day long."

William James said, "The greatest discovery of my generation is that **human beings can alter their lives by altering their attitudes of mind.**"

And he also said, "We need only in cold blood act as if the thing in question were real, and it will become infallibly real by growing into such a connection with our life that it will become real. It will become so knit with habit and emotion that our interests in it will be those which characterize belief."

He also said, "If you only care enough for a result,

you will almost certainly attain it. If you wish to be rich, you will be rich; if you wish to be learned, you will be learned; if you wish to be good, you will be good. Only you must, then, really wish these things, and wish them exclusively, and not wish at the same time a hundred other incompatible things just as strongly.

REFLECTION QUESTIONS

Ask Yourself...

1. Who do you personally know who seems to have "the magic touch"? Reflect on the goals this person has accomplished, and consider the trajectory of their success. What type of mindset or attitude does this individual maintain?

2. What do you spend your time thinking about? Do most of your thoughts have a positive or a negative tone?

3. Are your thoughts centered more on your own actions and feelings or on the actions and feelings of others?

The biggest mistake that you can make is to believe that you are working for somebody else. Job security is gone. The driving force of a career must come from the individual. Remember, jobs are owned by the company; you own your career!

—EARL NIGHTINGALE

3

BELIEVE AND SUCCEED

In the Bible, you'll read in Mark 9:23: "If thou canst believe, all things are possible to him that believeth."

My old friend, Dr. Norman Vincent Peale, put it this way: "This is one of the greatest laws in the universe, fervently do I wish I had discovered it as a very young man. It dawned upon me much later in life, and I have found it to be one of my greatest—if not my greatest— discovery, outside of my relationship to God... The great law briefly and simply stated is that if you think

Now, let's say that the farmer has two seeds in his hand—one is a seed of corn, the other is nightshade, a deadly poison. He digs two little holes in the earth, and he plants both seeds—one corn, the other nightshade. He covers up the holes, waters, and takes care of the land...and what will happen? Invariably, the land will return what was planted. As it's written in the Bible, "As ye sow, so shall ye reap."

Remember, the land doesn't care. It will return

poison in just as wonderful abundance as it will corn. So up come the two plants—one corn, one poison.

The human mind is far more fertile, far more incredible and mysterious than the land, but it works the same way. It doesn't care what we plant...success...or failure. A concrete, worthwhile goal...or confusion, misunderstanding, fear, anxiety, and so on. But what we plant it must return to us.

You see, **the human mind is the last great, unexplored continent on earth.** It contains riches beyond our wildest dreams. It will return anything we want to plant.

Now, you might say, if that's true, why don't people use their minds more? Well, I think they've figured out an answer to that one too. Our mind comes as standard equipment at birth. It's free. And things that are given to us for nothing, we place little value on. Things that we pay money for, we value.

The paradox is that exactly the reverse is true.

Everything that's really worthwhile in life came to us free—our minds, our souls, our bodies, our

Ask Yourself...

1. Reflect on the quote, "Our doubts are traitors and make us lose the good we oft might win by fearing to attempt." How often has fear prevented you from pursuing a goal?

2. If our minds—like the land—return to us what we plant, then our mindsets will reflect what we've consumed. Assess your current "mental harvest." What negative or oppressive messages might you be ingesting too frequently?

3. Define your measurable, specific goal.

All you have to do is know where you're going. The answers will come to you of their own accord.

—EARL NIGHTINGALE

4

YOU'RE IN THE DRIVER'S SEAT

Ours has been called the "phenobarbital age," the age of ulcers, nervous breakdowns, and tranquilizers. At a time when medical research has raised us to a new plateau of good health and longevity, far too many of us worry ourselves into an early grave trying to cope with things in our own little personal ways—without ever learning a few great laws that will take care of everything for us.

These things we bring on ourselves through our habitual way of thinking. Every one of us is the sum

Now, this information is enormously valuable to us if we really understand it and apply it. It's valuable to us not only for our own lives but the lives of those around us—our families, employees, associates, and friends.

Life should be an exciting adventure; it should never be a bore.

You should live fully—be alive.

You should be glad to get out of bed in the morning. You should be doing a job you like to do and because you do it well.

One time I heard Grove Patterson, the great, late editor-in-chief of the *Toledo Daily Blade*, make a speech. And as he concluded his speech, he said something I've never forgotten. He said, "My years in the newspaper business have convinced me of several things. Among them, that people are basically good and that we came from someplace and we're going someplace. So we should make our time here an exciting adventure."

The architect of the universe didn't build a stairway leading nowhere.

And the greatest teacher of all, the carpenter from the plains of Galilee, gave us the secret time and time again: "As ye believe, so shall it be done unto you."

I've explained what I call the strangest secret and how it works. Now I want to explain how you can prove to yourself the enormous returns possible in your own life by putting this secret to a practical test. I want to make a test that will last thirty days. It isn't going to be easy, but if you will give it a good try, **it will completely change your life for the better.**

Back in the seventeenth century, Sir Isaac Newton, the English mathematician and philosopher, gave us some natural laws of physics that apply as much to human beings as they do to the movement of bodies in the universe. And one of these laws is that for every action, there is an equal and opposite reaction. Simply stated, as it applies to you and me, it means we can achieve nothing without paying the price. The results of your thirty-day experiment will be in direct proportion to the effort you put forth.

REFLECTION QUESTIONS

Ask Yourself...

1. Do you tend to control your thinking, or does your thinking tend to control you?

2. Would you describe your life now as "an exciting adventure"? How might implementing the strangest secret make this a reality?

3. Reflect on how the law of cause and effect has been evidenced in your own life. Write down at least two examples: one good, one bad.

The more intensely we feel about an idea or a goal, the more assuredly the idea, buried deep in our subconscious, will direct us along the path to its fulfillment.

—EARL NIGHTINGALE

5

THE PRICE OF SUCCESS

To be a doctor, you must pay the price of long years of difficult study. To be successful in selling—and remember that each of us succeeds to the extent of his ability to sell: selling our families on our ideas, selling education in schools, selling our children on the advantages of living the good and honest life, selling our associates and employees on the importance of being exceptional people...also, of course, the profession of selling itself—to be successful in selling our way to the good life, **we must be willing to pay the price.**

Now, what is that price?

Well, it's many things:

First, it's understanding emotionally as well as intellectually that we literally become what we think about, that we must control our thoughts if we're to control our lives. It's understanding fully that "as ye sow, so shall ye reap."

Second, it's cutting away all fetters from the mind and permitting it to soar as it was divinely designed to do. It's the realization that your limitations are self-imposed and that the opportunities for you today are enormous beyond belief. It's rising above narrow-minded pettiness and prejudice.

Third, it's using all your courage to force yourself to think positively on your own problems, to set a definite and clearly defined goal for yourself. To let your marvelous mind think about your goal from all possible angles, to let your imagination speculate freely upon many different possible solutions. To refuse to believe that there are any circumstances sufficiently strong enough to defeat you in the accomplishment of your purpose. To act promptly and decisively when your course is clear. And to keep constantly aware of the fact that you are, at this moment, standing in the middle of your own "acre of diamonds," as Russell Conwell used to point out.

And fourth, save at least 10 percent of every dollar you earn.

It's also remembering that, no matter what your present job, it has enormous possibilities—if you're willing to pay the price by keeping these four points in mind:

 You will become what you think about.

 Remember the word *imagination* and let your mind begin to soar.

Courageously concentrate on your goal every day.

4 Save 10 percent of what you earn.

Finally, *take action*—ideas are worthless unless we act on them.

Now, I'll try to outline the thirty-day test I want you to take. Keep in mind that you have nothing to lose by taking this test...and everything you could possibly want to gain.

There are two things that may be said of everyone: Each of us wants something. And each of us is afraid of something.

I want you to write on a card what it is you want more than anything else.

It may be more money. Perhaps you'd like to double your income or make a specific amount of money. It may be a beautiful home. It may be success at your job. It may be a particular position in life. It could be a more harmonious family.

Abundance is yours for the asking.

Each of us wants something. Write down on your card specifically what it is you want. Make sure it's a single goal and clearly defined. You needn't show it to anyone, but carry it with you so that you can look at it several times a day. Think about it in a cheerful, relaxed, positive way each morning when you get up, and immediately **you have something to work for...something to get out of bed for...something to live for.**

Look at it every chance you get during the day and just before going to bed at night. And as you look at it, remember that you must become what you think about, and since you're thinking about your goal, you realize that soon, it will be yours. In fact, it's really yours the moment you write it down and begin to think about it.

Look at the abundance all around you as you go about your daily business. You have as much right to this abundance as any other living creature. It's yours for the asking.

Now we come to the difficult part—difficult because it means the formation of what is probably a brand new habit, and new habits are not easily formed. Once formed, however, it will follow you for the rest of your life.

Stop thinking about what it is you fear. Each time a fearful or negative thought comes into your consciousness, replace it with a mental picture of your positive and worthwhile goal. And there will come a time when you'll feel like giving up. It's easier for a human being to think negatively than positively. That's why only five percent are successful. You must begin now to place yourself in that group.

For thirty days, you must take control of your mind. It will think only about what you permit it to think about.

All you have to do is know where you're going.

Each day for this thirty-day test, do more than you have to do. In addition to maintaining a cheerful, positive outlook, give of yourself more than you have ever done before. Do this knowing that your returns in life must be in direct proportion to what you give.

The moment you decide on a goal to work toward, you're immediately a successful person. You are then in that rare and successful category of people who know where they're going. Out of every hundred people, you belong in the top five. Don't concern yourself too much with how you are going to achieve your goal—leave that completely to a power greater than yourself. All you have to do is know where you're going. The answers will come to you of their own accord and at the right time.

Remember these words from the Sermon on the Mount, and remember them well. Keep them constantly before you during this month of your test:

Ask, and it shall be given you; seek, and ye shall find; knock, and it shall be opened unto you. For everyone that asketh receiveth; and he that seeketh findeth; and to him that knocketh it shall be opened.

It's as marvelous and as simple as that. In fact, it's so simple that in our seemingly complicated world, it's difficult for an adult to understand that all he or she needs is a purpose...and faith!

For thirty days, do your very best.

No matter what your job, do it as you've never done it before for thirty days, and—if you've kept your goal before you every day—you'll wonder and marvel at this new life you've found.

Dorothea Brande, the outstanding editor and writer, discovered it for herself and tells about it in her fine book *Wake Up and Live.* Her entire philosophy is reduced to the words **"Act as though it were impossible to fail."**

She made her own test, with sincerity and faith, and her entire life was changed to one of overwhelming success.

Now, you make your test...for thirty full days. Don't start your test until you've made up your mind to stick with it. You see, by being persistent, you're

Ask Yourself...

1. Are you ready and willing to "pay the price" for success?

2. What fears may arise over the next thirty days? List those potential fears, and proactively consider how you can overcome them.

3. Which book will you read over the next thirty days to encourage you throughout the challenge?

Don't let the fear of the time it will take to accomplish something stand in the way of your doing it.

—EARL NIGHTINGALE

6

START TODAY

Now, since taking this test is difficult, some may say, "Why should I bother?" Well, look at the alternative! No one wants to be a failure; no one really wants to be a mediocre individual; no one wants a life constantly filled with worry, fear, and frustration.

Therefore, remember that you must reap that which you sow. If you sow negative thoughts, your life will be filled with negative things. If you sow positive thoughts, your life will be cheerful, successful, and positive.

Gradually, you will have a tendency to forget what you've read in this book. Read it often; keep reminding yourself of what you must do to form this new habit. Gather your whole family around at regular intervals and review what's been written here.

Most people will tell you that they want to make money without understanding this law. The only people who make money work in a mint. The rest of us must earn money. This is what causes those who keep looking for something for nothing, or a free ride, to fail in life.

The only way to earn money is by providing people with services or products that are needed and useful. We exchange our time and our product or service for the other person's money. Therefore, the law is that our financial return will be in direct proportion to our service.

Now, success is not the result of making money; making money is the result of success—and success is in direct proportion to our service.

Most people have this law backward. They believe that you're successful if you earn a lot of money. The truth is that you can only earn money after you're successful.

It's like the story of the man who sat in front of the stove and said to it, "Give me heat and then I'll add the wood."

How many men and women do you know or do you suppose there are today who take the same attitude toward life? There are millions.

We've got to put the fuel in before we can expect heat. Likewise, we've got to be of service first before we can expect money. Don't concern yourself with the money. **Be of service...build...work...dream...create!** Do this and you'll find there is no limit to the prosperity and abundance that will come to you.

Prosperity, you know, is founded upon a law of mutual exchange. Any person who contributes to prosperity must prosper, in turn, himself. Sometimes the return will not come from those you serve, but it must come to you from someplace, because that's the law.

For every action, there is an equal and opposite reaction.

As you go daily through your thirty-day test period, remember that your success will always be measured by the quality and quantity of service you render, and money is a yardstick for measuring this service.

No man can get rich himself unless he enriches others.

There are no exceptions to this law. You can drive down any street in America and from your car estimate the service that is being rendered by the people living on that street. Had you ever thought of this yardstick before? It's interesting. Some, like ministers and priests and other devoted people, measure their returns in the realm of the spiritual, but again, their returns are equal to their service.

Once this law is fully understood, any thinking person can tell his own fortune. If he wants more, he must be of more service to those from whom he receives his return. If he wants less, he has only to reduce this service. This is the price you must pay for what you want.

If you believe you can enrich yourself by deluding others, you can end only by deluding yourself. It may take some time, but just as surely as you breathe, you'll get back what you put out. Don't ever make the mistake of thinking you can avert this. It's impossible!

The prisons and the streets where the lonely walk are filled with people who tried to make new laws just for themselves. We may avoid the laws of man for a while. But there are greater laws that cannot be broken.

An outstanding medical doctor once pointed out six steps that will help you realize success:

 Set yourself a definite goal.

Quit running yourself down.

Stop thinking of all the reasons why you cannot be successful, and instead, think of all the reasons why you can.

 Trace your attitudes back through your childhood, and try to discover where you first got the idea you couldn't be successful, if that's the way you've been thinking.

 Change the image you have of yourself by writing out a description of the person you would like to be.

 Act the part of the successful person you have decided to become!

The doctor who wrote those words is the noted West Coast psychiatrist Dr. David Harold Fink.

Do what experts since the dawn of recorded history have told you you must do: pay the price by becoming the person you want to become. It's not nearly as difficult as living unsuccessfully.

Take your thirty-day test, then repeat it…then repeat it again. Each time, it will become more a part of you until you'll wonder how you could have ever have lived any other way. Live this new way, and the floodgates of abundance will open and pour over you more riches than you may have dreamed existed. Money? Yes, lots of it.

But what's more important, you'll have peace. You'll be in that wonderful minority who lead calm, cheerful, successful lives.

Start today. You have nothing to lose—but you have a whole life to win.

This is Earl Nightingale…and thank you.

REFLECTION QUESTIONS

Ask Yourself...

1. How will you continually remind yourself of the strangest secret?

2. In what ways can you be of more service to others in your workplace? Family? Community?

3. Visualize and write down a clear description of the person you want to become. When you feel discouraged, return to this visual of your future self for motivation.

Learn to enjoy every minute of your life. Be happy now. Don't wait for something outside of yourself to make you happy in the future. Think how really precious is the time you have to spend, whether it's at work or with your family. Every minute should be enjoyed and savored.

—EARL NIGHTINGALE

Take the
30-DAY
Challenge

Start today. You have nothing to lose, but you have your whole life to win.

—EARL NIGHTINGALE

STEP 1: Now that you've read _The Strangest Secret_, identify how you can improve.

Jot down five practices you can apply to your life, starting right now, that you aren't currently doing.

Small or large, how can you be doing more for yourself and your goals?

STEP 2: Write down one specific goal.

Take a few minutes and decide upon the one goal that you most want to tackle. Make sure it's a single goal, clearly detailed and defined. Write this goal down on a small piece of paper, and carry it with you for the next thirty days, looking at it several times each day. In Earl's own words, **"Think about it in a cheerful, relaxed, positive way each morning when you get up, and immediately you have something to work for…something to get out of bed for…something to live for."**

STEP 3: Move beyond your fear.

As Earl himself said, **"Stop thinking about what it is you fear. Each time a fearful or negative thought comes to your mind, replace it with a mental picture of your positive and worthwhile goal."**

Fear is nothing more than a distraction from your life's calling. Which will you choose: to succumb to the fear that holds you back or to boldly step into the life you deserve?

STEP 4: Be of service.

The old adage "it's better to give than receive" actually contains a valuable truth. Earl says it like this: **"Your success will always be measured by the quality and quantity of service you render. We've got to be of service before we can expect a return."**

For the next thirty days, focus on serving those around you with your time, energy, and emotion. You'll be amazed at how much this benevolence fuels your own potential for growth.

Don't start until you are ready.

But don't let fear stop you!

There will never be a better time to begin than today, so why wait? Experience the power of the strangest secret in your own life.

Step 5: Repeat!

Once one goal is accomplished, another idea should hatch!

Take this thirty-day challenge, then repeat it again and again. Each time, it will become a more vital part of your life until you'll wonder how you ever lived another way. Earl advised, **"live this new way, and the floodgates of abundance will open and pour over you more riches than you may have dreamed existed. Money? Yes, lots of it. But what's more important, you'll have peace."**

Recommended
READING

THE LEGACY JOURNEY   Dave Ramsey

How many of us struggle to find the balance between increasing our wealth and finding joy and contentedness with what we already have? Providing a comprehensive biblical perspective on wealth, monetary growth, and, ultimately, financial peace, *The Legacy Journey* is a "can't miss" read for anyone seeking a faith-based approach to finances.

LIVE YOUR DREAMS   Les Brown

Filled with incredible wisdom, examples, and even an Action Planner, Les's personal formula for success and happiness is a tool that every individual should have in their arsenal. The perfect complement to Earl Nightingale's inspiring messages, *Live Your Dreams* will empower you on the path to goal realization.

LIMITLESS: UNLEASHING YOUR WEALTH   Earl Nightingale

If someone asked you how much money you wanted, what would you say? Here's the deeper question: how much money are your contributions worth? In this compelling message, Nightingale shares the secrets to unleashing limitless wealth.

YOUR GRASS IS GREENER   Earl Nightingale

We've all heard the old cliché that the grass is greener on the other side…but what if the grass you're already standing on is the greenest of all? Learn how to recognize and capitalize on the opportunities you already have in *Your Grass is Greener.*

WIN TODAY, WIN TOMORROW, WIN ALWAYS   Earl Nightingale

Ever had a goal that felt too far out of reach? Ever wondered what it would take to step into the life of success you've dreamed of? In this insightful message, Nightingale reveals the key to ensuring that you achieve consistent success in any area—today, tomorrow, and always.

WHO'S THE BOSS?   Earl Nightingale

We all have the same boss—and their identity might surprise you. In *Who's The Boss?*, Nightingale unveils the formula to increasing our rewards by recognizing who we're truly serving.

About the
AUTHOR

© Nightingale Legacy

EARL NIGHTINGALE knew a thing or two about overcoming obstacles and conquering difficulties, and he had a unique gift for inspiring those around him to do the same. Born into a poor California family in 1921, Earl survived the meager years of the

Depression, joined the Marines at age seventeen, and was one of only twelve men to survive the Pearl Harbor bombing of the battleship USS *Arizona*. After leaving the service, he embarked on a career in broadcasting. His sonorous voice and articulate, impassioned delivery won him great acclaim in the broadcasting industry. At the insurance company he purchased at the height of his radio career, the sales force relied on his regular Saturday pep talks, delivered over the PA system, to motivate their performance through the week. One week in 1956, Earl prerecorded his message so that he could take a vacation without his staff missing their weekly dose of inspiration. The message absolutely electrified the staff. Word of this extraordinary recording spread, and the office was soon deluged with requests for a copy of it. To keep pace, Earl recorded the message, which he called *The Strangest Secret*, on ten-inch records. Within a year, through nothing more than word-of-mouth, they were selling two thousand copies a week.

In 1960, Earl Nightingale cofounded the Nightingale-Conant corporation to distribute this information. Since then, the audio version of *The Strangest Secret* has sold well over a million copies and continues to improve the lives of everyone it touches.

NEW! Only from Simple Truths®

IGNITE READS
spark impact in just one hour

IGNITE READS IS A NEW SERIES OF 1-HOUR READS WRITTEN BY WORLD-RENOWNED EXPERTS!

These captivating books will help you become the best version of yourself, allowing for new opportunities in your personal and professional life. Accelerate your career and expand your knowledge with these powerful books written on today's hottest ideas.

TRENDING BUSINESS AND PERSONAL GROWTH TOPICS

 Read in an hour or less

 Leading experts and authors

 Bold design and captivating content